I0817430

FOODS FROM
UKRAINE
MARY SHAW
childsworld.com

Published by The Child's World®
800-599-READ · www.childsworld.com

Photography Credits
Photographs ©: Oleksandra Naumenko/Shutterstock Images, cover (background), 1 (background), 3 (background); Shutterstock Images, cover (flag), 1 (flag), 3 (flag), 4 (flag), 5 (globe), 17, 18–19, 20, 22; Boyko Pictures/ Shutterstock Images, 4 (landmarks), back cover; Peter Hermes Furian/Shutterstock Images, 5 (country); Galina Sandalova/iStockphoto, 6–7; iStockphoto, 8, 12; Marian Curko/Shutterstock Images, 11; Tereza Koudelkova/ Shutterstock Images, 14–15

ISBN Information
9781503885332 (Reinforced Library Binding)
9781503885707 (Portable Document Format)
9781503886346 (Online Multi-user eBook)
9781503886988 (Electronic Publication)

LCCN 2023937429

Printed in the United States of America

Mary Shaw writes, edits, and designs children's books. She lives in Minnesota with her partner and their two cats. She has been cooking traditional Ukrainian food with her mother since she was a child. Both of them hope to share a meal with family and friends in Ukraine again soon.

TABLE OF CONTENTS

UKRAINE

Ukraine is the second-largest country in Europe. It borders seven other countries. Ukrainian winters are usually cold and snowy. Summers are hot and rainy. Crimea is a **peninsula** in southern Ukraine. It is surrounded by the Black Sea. Its southern coast is warm.

Each part of Ukraine has its own type of **cuisine**. Fish is a **staple** in southern Ukrainian cooking. Mushrooms are **foraged** in the Carpathian Mountains. Ukrainians use them in soups, dumplings, and sauces. **Crimean Tatars** popularized grilled meats in southern Ukraine.

Ukraine is known as the breadbasket of Europe. This is because its soil is perfect for growing grain. Many recipes use grains such as wheat, barley, and buckwheat. Potatoes and other root vegetables, such as beets, are commonly used. Ukrainians even use bread and beets to make sweet drinks, such as *kvass* (KVAHZ)!

Ukrainians cook big feasts for holidays. For Easter, Ukrainians make a sweet bread called *paska* (PAH-skah). It is tall and round, with icing and colorful sprinkles.

BORSCH

Beets are a staple in Ukrainian cooking. They give *borsch* (BORSH-ch) its bright-red color. Borsch is beet soup. There are many different recipes for this soup. It can be made with fish, oxtail or other cuts of beef, or chicken. It can also be made without meat.

To make borsch, cooks dice or **grate** vegetables. These include beets, carrots, cabbage, potatoes, onions, celery, and garlic. The beets are **sautéed** in a large pot. Then broth and water are added. So are the carrots, cabbage, and potatoes.

Borsch is traditionally served in clay or wooden dishes.

Many vegetables go into borsch.

BORSCH IN SPACE

Borsch has been eaten in space since the 1960s. Astronauts used to eat it out of a metal tube. Today, astronauts still enjoy the Ukrainian soup. Astronaut Randy Bresnik ate borsch while living on the International Space Station.

The onion, celery, and garlic are fried in a frying pan. Tomato paste adds extra flavor and color. The fried vegetables are added to the boiling broth. Kidney beans and bay leaves go in the pot, too. So does meat, if it is being used.

The last step is adding seasonings. These include salt, pepper, and fresh dill. The soup boils until the flavors are fully mixed together. This traditional dish is usually served with sour cream and dill as a **garnish**. Borsch tastes sweet and slightly sour. *Pampushky* (pahm-POOH-shkih) is a garlic bread roll. It is usually served on the side.

HOLUBTSI

Ukrainian cabbage rolls are called *holubtsi* (HOL-oob-tsee). The name translates to "little pigeons." Steamed cabbage leaves are rolled around a filling. This filling typically has buckwheat and ground meat. There are also spices and vegetables.

Holubtsi are cabbage rolls often served in tomato sauce.

Holubtsi are usually stuffed with grain and meat.

AROUND THE WORLD WITH CABBAGE ROLLS

Many different cultures eat stuffed cabbage rolls. In Egypt, they are thin. They are filled with Arabic spices and fresh herbs. In Balkan countries, the rolls are simmered between layers of sauerkraut. Chinese stuffed cabbage rolls can be filled with shiitake mushrooms. They are dipped in oyster sauce.

To make cabbage rolls, cooks boil cabbage leaves. This makes them soft enough to roll. Next, vegetables are fried in a pan with oil. Onions and carrots are commonly used. Tomato paste, sugar, and bay leaves are added. Then diced tomatoes and water are added. Together, the ingredients make a rich sauce. The rolls cook in this sauce. Sometimes cooks make a mushroom sauce instead.

Next, the meat and cooked buckwheat or rice are mixed in a bowl with chopped onion. The mixture is seasoned with salt, paprika, and parsley.

Though they are now an everyday food, holubtsi were once served only for special occasions such as Christmas or weddings.

Then cooks assemble the cabbage rolls. The cabbage leaves are filled with two spoonfuls of the filling. The sides of the leaves are folded. Then the holubtsi are rolled like small burritos. The finished rolls are stacked in the pot of tomato sauce. Cooks put a lid on the pot. The rolls cook in the steam. Holubtsi are usually topped with sour cream and dill. Bread is served on the side.

CHERRY VARENYKY

Varenyky (vah-REH-nih-kih) are boiled dumplings. The name comes from the Ukrainian word *varýty*. This means "to boil." The dumplings can have many different fillings. **Savory** fillings can make a **hearty** dinner. But these dumplings can also be a dessert. Cherry dumplings are traditionally made in the summertime. This is when cherries are ready to be picked. Fresh or frozen cherries can be used all year round.

Sweet cheese, cherries, or other fruits are possible stuffings for sweet varenyky.

The dumpling dough is made with eggs, butter, milk, and flour. Some people use premade dough. Wonton wrappers make a good substitute. Once the dough is prepared, the cherries are pitted. Pitting a cherry is removing the hard seed, or pit, in the middle. The cherries are then mixed with sugar and cornstarch.

Once the dough is made, cooks make the dumplings. Before starting, cooks sprinkle flour on a countertop or table. Then they roll out the dough. Next, cooks cut circles from the dough. Many use a cookie cutter or an upside-down glass. This keeps the dough circles the same size. Each circle is filled with about three cherries. Then the dough is folded in half. Cooks tightly pinch along the edges. This makes sure the cherry mixture does not leak.

Making varenyky in a group helps the process take less time.

Sour cream or whipped cream can be used to top varenyky.

Then the dumplings are cooked. A pot of water and sugar is brought to a boil. The dumplings are gently added to the pot. They boil for only a few minutes. Once cooked, the dumplings go into a bowl. Cooks add butter so they do not stick. Finally, sugar is sprinkled all over for added sweetness. Ukrainians traditionally eat varenyky with sour cream. But a dollop of whipped cream can be added instead.

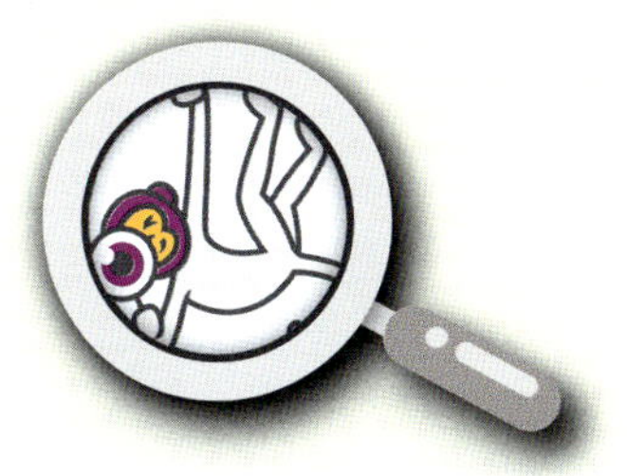

WONDER MORE

Wondering about New Information

How much did you know about Ukrainian cuisine before reading this book? What new information did you learn? Write down three new facts you learned from this book. Was the new information surprising? Why or why not?

Wondering How It Matters

Why do you think it is important to learn about foods from different countries? How can learning about and trying new foods affect your life? Are there any foods from Ukraine you would like to try?

Wondering Why

Ukrainian food is prepared in many different ways across the country. Why do you think dishes are prepared differently depending on the area where they are made?

Ways to Keep Wondering

After reading this book, what questions do you have about Ukrainian food? What can you do to learn more about it?

CHERRY VARENYKY RECIPE

Making varenyky dough is tricky. With an adult's help, try making this simpler version using wonton wrappers.

Ingredients

- ½ pound pitted dark cherries, fresh or thawed from frozen
- ½ cup granulated sugar, divided
- 1 package (about 20) wonton wrappers
- Flour for dusting
- 1 tablespoon cornstarch
- 2 tablespoons unsalted butter, melted
- Sour cream or whipped cream (optional)

Steps

1. Combine cherries, ¼ cup sugar, and cornstarch in a bowl. Stir gently.
2. Place separated wonton wrappers on a lightly floured surface. Spoon 2 to 3 cherries into the center of each wrapper. Then fold the circle in half to create a semicircle. Dip fingers in water and lightly pinch the edges to seal.
3. Bring a large pot of water and 2 tablespoons of sugar to boil. Drop the dumplings into the boiling water. Stir with a spoon to prevent them from sticking. Cook for 5 to 7 minutes. When the dumplings float to the top, they are done. Use a wire skimmer or a wide cooking spoon to lift the dumplings out of the water and into a large bowl.
4. Coat the dumplings with butter and sprinkle with the remaining sugar. Serve immediately, topped with sour cream or whipped cream if desired.

GLOSSARY

Crimean Tatars (kry-MEE-un tah-TARZ) Crimean Tatars are an ethnic group and nation native to Crimea. Grilled meats were introduced by Crimean Tatars and are popular across Ukraine.

cuisine (kwih-ZEEN) A cuisine is a style of cooking. Grains and root vegetables are an important part of Ukrainian cuisine.

foraged (FOR-ijd) Foraged foods have been found and collected from nature. Foraged mushrooms can be used in soups and sauces.

garnish (GAR-nish) A garnish is an ingredient placed on top of a meal for decoration or extra flavor. Dill is a common Ukrainian garnish.

grate (GRAYT) To grate food is to rub it against something sharp to create small pieces. Cooks grate vegetables for borsch.

hearty (HAR-tee) Something that is hearty is filling and rich. Varenyky can make a hearty dinner or a sweet dessert.

peninsula (puh-NIN-soo-luh) A peninsula sticks out from the mainland and is surrounded by water. Crimea is a peninsula.

sautéed (saw-TAYD) When food is sautéed, it is fried in a hot pan with butter or oil. Beets are sautéed before being added to borsch.

savory (SAY-vuh-ree) When a food is savory, it tastes salty or spicy. Varenyky can be sweet or savory.

staple (STAY-puhl) A staple food is one that people eat almost every day. Beets and other root vegetables are a staple of Ukrainian cuisine.

FIND OUT MORE

In the Library

Kesselring, Susan, and Elisa Chavarri. *National Day Traditions around the World.* Parker, CO: The Child's World, 2022.

Spanier, Kristine. *Ukraine.* Minneapolis, MN: Jump!, 2023.

Vasilyeva, Anastasiya. *Ukraine.* New York, NY: Bearport Publishing, 2017.

On the Web

Visit our website for links about foods from Ukraine:
childsworld.com/links

Note to Parents, Caregivers, Teachers, and Librarians: We routinely verify our Web links to make sure they are safe and active sites. So encourage your readers to check them out!

INDEX